# TODAY'S  SCRIBES

_____

_(your name)_

# Anointed to Write

## Journal/ Workbook

Dr. Janet Shuler

ISBN-13: 978-1986739511
ISBN-10: 1986739511

# Dedication:

To God's scribes everywhere – WRITE and do not hold back! May revelation, healing and joy flow to you and through you as you write.
Study to show yourself approved.

Glorify the Father. As you lift Him up He will lift you up!

May you find your voice, and experience personal fulfillment, satisfaction as your expression is released in writing.

# CONTENTS

## ACKNOWLEDEGEMENT

Thank you Stephanie Pagan Guridy for your prophetic painting entitled, "Richness and Fullness in the Depth" seen on the front cover. Stephanie is a young artist currently residing in NYC. This painting was created during worship, as an act of prophetic worship at Breakthrough Culture in Times Square, a church under Apostle Torrey Marcel Harper.

## INTRODUCTION

You have a story to tell, a voice to be heard, wisdom to be shared, and more. The power of the pen is mighty and YOU are loaded with purpose! Unlock your potential as a writer, and learn the basics of becoming a published author! This is your year – walk through the open door and into new beginnings!

This workbook is ideal as an accompaniment with the course, 'Anointed to Write 101' by Dr. Janet Shuler. The course may be taken on site, in person or is also available online. Visit **www.jshuler.blog** or email Dr. Janet at HKMdrJanet@gmail.com .

Whether you do or don't take the course, this workbook is certain to be a motivational springboard into writing.

Enjoy! And WRITE, for such a time as this!

# 1 SCRIPTURES ON SCRIBES, WORDS & WRITING

*Note the insights, revelation, inspiration and/or instruction you glean from these verses.*

Exodus 17:14-15 Then the LORD said to Moses, "Write this on a scroll as something to be remembered and make sure that Joshua hears it, because I will completely blot out the name of Amalek from under heaven." Moses built an altar and called it The LORD is my Banner.

_____

_____

_____

_____

_____

Exodus 34:27-28 Then the LORD said to Moses, "Write down these words, for in accordance with these words I have made a covenant with you and with Israel." Moses was there with the LORD forty days and forty nights without eating bread or drinking water. And he wrote on the tablets the words of the covenant—the Ten Commandments.

_____

_____

_____

_____

_____

Deuteronomy 6:9, Dt. 11:20 Write them on the doorframes of your house and on your gates.

_____

_____

_____

_____

_____

Deuteronomy 29:29 The secret things belong to the LORD our God, but the things revealed belong to us and to our children forever, that we may follow all the words of this law.

_____

_____

_____

_____

_____

Deuteronomy 32:2 Let my teaching fall like rain and my words descend like dew, like showers on new grass, like abundant rain on tender plants.

_____

_____

_____

_____

_____

2 Chronicles 34:13 Some of the Levites were secretaries, scribes and gatekeepers.

_____

_____

_____

Jeremiah 8:8 "'How can you say, "We are wise, for we have the law of the LORD," when actually the lying pen of the scribes has handled it falsely?

_____

_____

_____

_____

_____

Habakkuk 2:2-3
"Write down the revelation

and make it plain on tablets

so that a herald may run with it.

[3] For the revelation awaits an appointed time;

it speaks of the end

and will not prove false.

Though it linger, wait for it;

it will certainly come

and will not delay.

_____

_____

_____

_____

_____

_____

Proverbs 3:3-4

Let love and faithfulness never leave you;

bind them around your neck,

write them on the tablet of your heart.

Then you will win favor and a good name

in the sight of God and man.

_____

_____

_____

_____

_____

Proverbs 16:24 Gracious words are a honeycomb, sweet to the soul and
healing to the bones.

_____

_____

_____

_____

Proverbs 18:21 The tongue has the power of life and death,
and those who love it will eat its fruit.

_____

_____

_____

_____

_____

Luke 1:3  With this in mind, since I myself have carefully investigated everything from the beginning, I too decided to write an orderly account for you, most excellent Theophilus,

_____

_____

_____

_____

_____

2 Peter 3:16 "He writes the same way in all his letters, speaking in them of these matters. His letters contain some things that are hard to understand, which ignorant and unstable people distort, as they do the other Scriptures, to their own destruction."

_____

_____

_____

_____

_____

1 John 2:20-21 "But you have an anointing from the Holy One, and all of you know the truth. I do not write to you because you do not know the truth, but because you do know it and because no lie comes from the truth."

_____

_____

_____

_____

_____

Jude 2-4 Dear friends, although I was very eager to write to you about the salvation we share, I felt compelled to write and urge you to contend for the faith that was once for all entrusted to God's holy people. For certain individuals whose condemnation was written about long ago have secretly slipped in among you.

_____

_____

_____

_____

_____

Revelation 1:19 "Write, therefore, what you have seen, what is now and what will take place later.

_____

_____

_____

_____

_____

## 2  WRITING PROMPTS AND ACTIVATIONS

1.  What is your favorite book?

    _____

    _____

    Take the first sentence of your favorite book and make it the first
    sentence of your post.

    _____

    _____

    _____

    _____

    _____

    _____

2.  What is your favorite Bible

    verse?_____ Why?

    _____

    _____

    _____

    _____

    Give an example of a personal connection you have to it.

    _____

    _____

    _____

    _____

    _____

    _____

3.  Close your eyes and be still. What do you hear? Describe what you
    are hearing.

    _____

    _____

    _____

    _____

    _____

    _____

4. Who has been the most significant influence in your life *in a positive way* (a real person).

_____ _____

Why were they influential?

_____

_____

_____

Describe them.

_____

_____

_____

_____

_____

_____

_____

5. Who has been the most significant influence in your *life in a negative way* (a real person).

_____

Why were they influential?

_____

_____

Describe them.

_____

_____

_____

_____

_____

_____

6. If you were to be an animal what animal would you be?

_____

Why?

_____

_____

Describe an episode/or an event as that animal.

_____

_____

_____

_____

_____

_____

7.  Write a Haiku (3 unrhymed lines. 1st line has 5 syllables, 2nd line has
    7 syllables, 3rd line has 5 syllables

    _____

    _____

    _____

    _____

8.  Step outside. Take a picture of the first thing you see. Go inside.
    Take a picture of the second thing you see. Write about the
    connection of these 2 random objects, people, or things.

    _____

    _____

    _____

    _____

    _____

    _____

    _____

9.  Technical writing. Pick one and write a how-to: (a) tying your shoe,
    (b) frying an egg (c) changing a diaper, (d) changing a light bulb (e)
    how to insert a gif in a text message.

    _____

    _____

    _____

    _____

    _____

    _____

    _____

10. Write a glowing 1 paragraph bio on yourself.

_____

_____

_____

_____

_____

_____

_____

11. Go to the nearest window. Look out and observe for a full minute. Write about what you saw.

_____

_____

_____

_____

_____

_____

_____

12. What is your favorite song? Pick a verse from it and write about your personal connection to it or what it means to you.

_____

_____

_____

_____

_____

_____

13. Give your life a title for an autobiography. What would your title be? Why?

_____

_____

_____

_____

_____

14. What smell reminds you of your childhood? Why? Describe that smell and a scene associated with it.

_____

_____

_____

_____

_____

_____

15. Your home is on fire. All people and pets are safe. Grab 5 items to take with you. What will they be? Why?

_____

_____

_____

_____

_____

_____

16. Here is an invented word: bishta. Define and use it in a post.

_____

_____

_____

_____

_____

_____

17. In the Torah it says, 'what comes from the heart, touches the heart'. Out of our deepest experiences and feelings come some of our best writings. Write about:
a) A time you were afraid
b) The saddest situation you were in
c) Most embarrassing moment/situation
d) Your happiest memory

e) a memory or emotion of your choice

_____

_____

_____

_____

_____

_____

_____

_____

_____

18. When was the last time someone told you they were proud of you?

_____

_____

_____

_____

_____

_____

_____

19. You can buy a plot of land anywhere you want. Money is not a problem. Describe where you'll buy the plot and what you'll do with it. _____

_____

_____

_____

_____

_____

20. What was your very first thought this morning?

_____

_____

_____

_____

_____

21. Pick a random letter from the alphabet and write about it.

_____

_____

_____

_____

_____

_____

_____

22. Here are 14 movie titles. Pick _one_ to use as the title of your autobiography. Write a post about that.
Back to the Future, Casa Blanca, Groundhog Day, Field of Dreams, American Pie, The Good, The Bad, and The Ugly; Coming to America, Daddy's Home, Transformers, Braveheart, Catch Me If You Can, Slumdog Millionaire, Dances With Wolves, Dog Day Afternoon. _____

_____

_____

_____

_____

_____

_____

23. Pick a controversial issue or topic that you are passionate about.
a) Write a post defending the _opposing_ viewpoint.

_____

_____

_____

_____

_____

_____

b) Write a post to convince someone of _your_ viewpoint.

_____

_____

_____

_____

_____

_____

_____

24. Think of your favorite teacher. What was their name? Why were you're your favorite? Recall and post a specific memory you have of them.

_____

_____

_____

_____

_____

_____

_____

25. You have won $3 million dollars. The condition of winning is that you must give all of it away except you may keep $1,000 for yourself. How/who will you give to? Why? And what will you do with the $1,000 that is yours?

_____

_____

_____

_____

_____

_____

_____

26. Revisit Prompt # 20. Elaborate upon it and extend your thoughts.

_____

_____

_____

_____

_____

_____

_____

27. Find a post or a quote on social media that grabs your attention. What is it? Elaborate and make personal connections.

_____

_____

_____

_____

_____

_____

_____

28. Who is your favorite fictional character? Why? Describe them.

_____

_____

_____

_____

_____

_____

_____

29. Tell about a journey – a physical trip or an emotional one that you took.

_____

_____

_____

_____

_____

_____

_____

30. You have the opportunity to rename yourself. What would you name yourself? Why?

_____

_____

_____

_____

_____

_____

_____

_____

31.The following are 6 samples of surrealism in art. Write about 1 or all of these picture prompts separately.

a.   By Anton Semenov aka Gloom82 from Bratsk, Russia

b. Vladimir Kush surrealism (and c also)

c.

d.

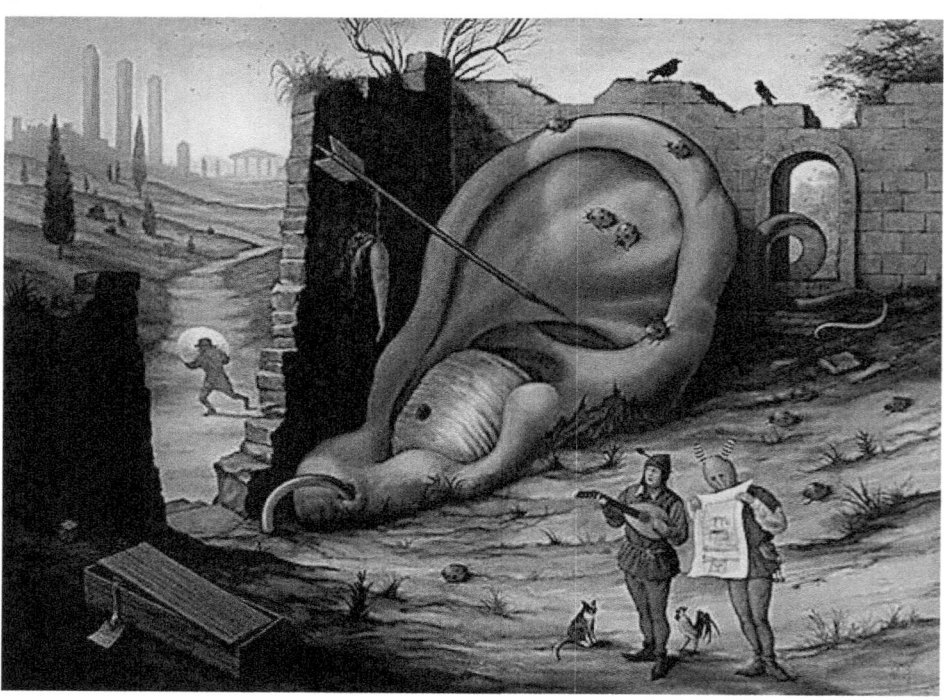

e.

f.

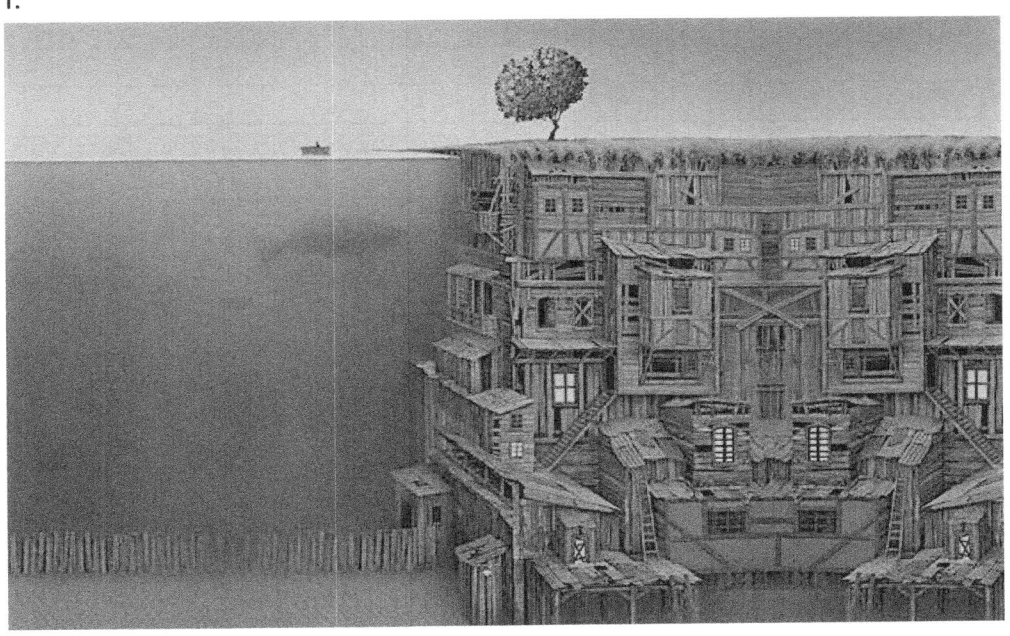

31. Select a picture of your own. (It may be a photograph, portrait, work of art, etc.) Copy, cut & paste it here. Why is this picture special to you? Why did you select this photo? How does it make you feel? Who is in this picture? What is happening in this picture? Write about it.

_____
_____
_____
_____
_____
_____

Dr. Janet Shuler

# 3   WRITERS CRAFT

What genre do you find yourself writing in most often? Which is your 'favorite' or preference? Stretch yourself and 'just for fun' write a bit in different genres. Keep yourself fresh and challenge your skills.

| GENRES | |
| --- | --- |
| **Fiction** | **Non-Fiction** |
| Action adventure, Super-heroes | Auto-Biography, Biography - someone's real life story (auto = the author's) |
| Comics - comic magazine, sequence of pictures | Essay - short composition that incl. the author's point of view or outlook |
| Comedy, humor | Journalism (reporting)- objective reporting, usually incl. who, what, when, where, why and how (5 W's and the H) |
| Crime/ detective, Mystery Thriller – a story that creates suspense and deals with finding the solution | Owners Manual (technical writing) how to, often includes diagrams |
| Fable, folklore, tall tale, fairy tale | Lab Report (experiment) |
| Mythology legend based in part on historical events, often about human behavior | Self-help book – coaching, advice, personal growth, etc. |
| Fantasy, paranormal – fiction with sub-plots, themes, major & minor characters | Diary, Travel Log – daily entries about one's life experiences/ travel experiences |
| Historical Fiction (story that is true to the life of a particular time period), realistic fiction – story that is true to life | Memoir – factual account that focuses on a specific, significant relationship between the writer and a person, place or an object |
|  |  |

| Fiction cont'd | Non-Fiction cont'd. |
|---|---|
| Science fiction – story based on the impact of actual or imagined events, often takes place in the future or another planet | Narrative, Personal Narrative – factual information about a significant event that reads like a story |
| Western | Speech |
| Children's literature, picture book | Reference, research |
| Romance | Critique |
| Short story – fiction of great brevity, usually supports, no sub-plots | Cook Book |
| Poetry | Poetry |

**Generating ideas, brainstorming and organizing** our thoughts can be challenging at times. Before we start writing we need to decide what we're writing about and how to organize our thoughts.

Spending time in prayer and in God's presence is the best means of getting revelation and clarity. There are some practical things we can do also, like: listing, chunking, etc. These graphic organizers may be helpful.

WORD STORM:
On the next page practice 'word association'. You may do this independently or with a small group of people. If you want fresh random ideas begin with whatever comes to your mind. If you aim is to get fresh approaches or perspective on a topic you're already working on then start by putting that word on the page and let contributions evolve. Simply jot down any and all words associated with that word that come to mind. One word may prompt an association of a new, different and totally unrelated word. Continue until you have a variety of words on the page.

# WORD STORM
(May be worked on independently or with a small group. Have fun!)

## MIND MAPPING

All Mind Maps have some things in common. They have a natural organizational structure that radiates from the center and use lines, symbols, words, colors and or images categorizing and connecting ideas. Mind Mapping is particularly helpful for visual learners. See samples below.

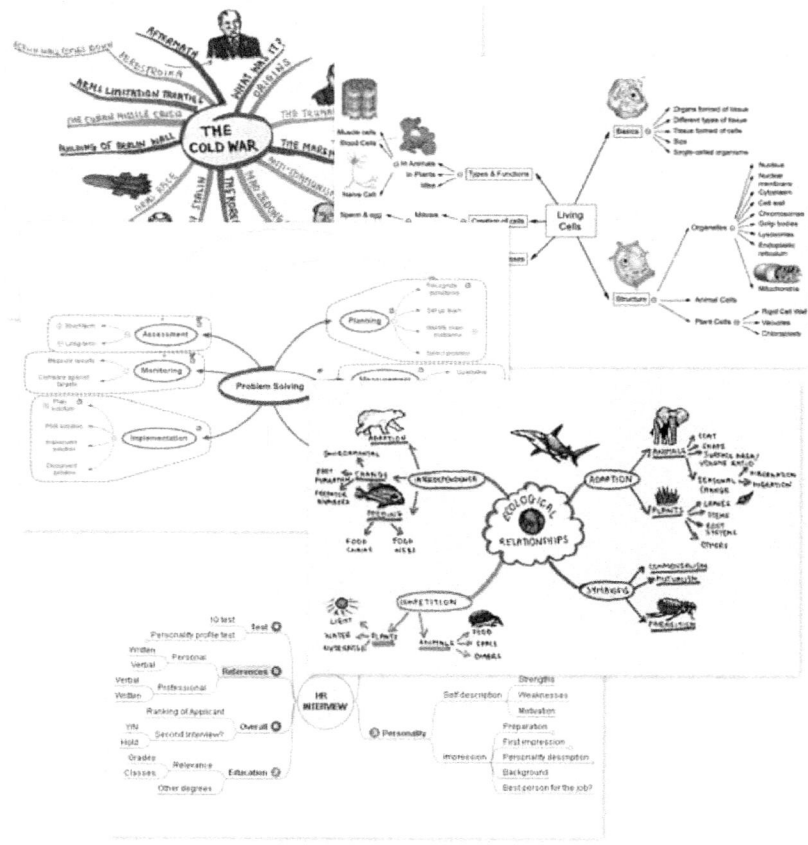

(There are also "mind mapping software" programs available.) Use the next page to do some mind mapping. *Suggestion – use pencil.* 6 Basics of Mind Mapping are:

1. Start from the center with a picture or 1 word of your main idea
2. The main themes radiate from the central image as 'branches'. (Using different colors for the branches can be visually helpful.)
3. The branches are sub-themes that radiate like spider webs. Label your branches/sub-themes
4. Topics of lesser importance are represented as 'twigs' of the relevant

branch.
5. Use short phrases or single words on the 'twigs'. Add images if they help get thoughts across better.
6. Try to think of at least 2 main points for each sub-theme, extend branches & twigs to them as appropriate.

...................................................................................................

MIND MAP

Dr. Janet Shuler

CHUNKING is getting your ideas out of your head, and organizing them by relationship. Here are some basics of 'chunking':

1. <u>Capture</u>: Get all of the ideas swimming in your head out and onto paper in one word or short phrase notations. (To-do lists, important people, themes, etc.) Think of this as a 'dumping ground' for your thoughts.
2. <u>Mark</u> the items that are essentials or very important. (Either circle or with an asterisk.)
3. <u>Chunk</u> what you've captured: Look for commonalities of the items that you've 'captured'. Some commonalities may be relationships, school, church, chapters, etc. (It's your list, you create the categories by how they are relevant to you.)

..................................................................................................................................

Use this page and p.31 to Capture and Mark. Then Chunk into the organizer on p. 32

CAPTURE & MARK

Dr. Janet Shuler

CAPTURE & MARK

# CHUNK

<u>Chunk</u> what you've captured: Look for commonalities of the items that you've 'captured'. Some commonalities may be relationships, school, church, chapters, etc. (It's your list, you create the categories by how they are relevant to you.)

| *Category:* | *Category:* |
|---|---|
| | |

| *Category:* | *Category:* |
|---|---|
| | |

| *Category:* | *Category:* |
|---|---|
| | |

*Chunking is a great strategy to use for organizing writing ideas and to order & schedule our personal life as well.*

**CUBING** is a writing exercise used as a pre-writing technique. Cubing, forces a writer to think and re-think a topic, allows a writer to explore various aspects of that topic. It may help you discover the most interesting aspect of your topic giving you a good start to focusing on your topic.

If you've never 'cubed' before you may want to use a concrete, physical object (a paperweight or a nick-knack). Look at it, write about what you see for 2 minutes. Then rotate to a different angle and write again for 2 minutes. Do this from 6 distinct vantage points.

Or, begin by writing about your topic.

- Time your writing with a clock or timer so that you write about six aspects of your topic for equal amounts of time. (Anywhere from 2-5 minutes)
- Push yourself to write about at least six views of your topic even if you can only think of three or four initially.
- Even if you think you know what your topic, position or thesis statement will be, try cubing for a few minutes.

The diagram on p. 34 is useful when cubing on a topic.

# Cube Template

Describe it...

Helpful prompts...
1. Describe: What does it taste, smell, feel, look like?
2. Compare: What is it similar to? What is it different from?
3. Associate: What does it make you think of?
4. Analyze: How is it made? How does it work?
5. Apply: How does it fit into your experience? How can you use it?
6. Argue: Is it positive or negative? Helpful or harmful?

Compare it...

Analyze it...

Associate it...

Apply it...

Argue for or against it...

This graphic organizer is by Frayer. One of my weaknesses is that I get side-tracked with extraneous or off-topic details. Using this Frayer organizer after some of the brainstorming we've already covered will help hone and fine tune your coverage of a topic.

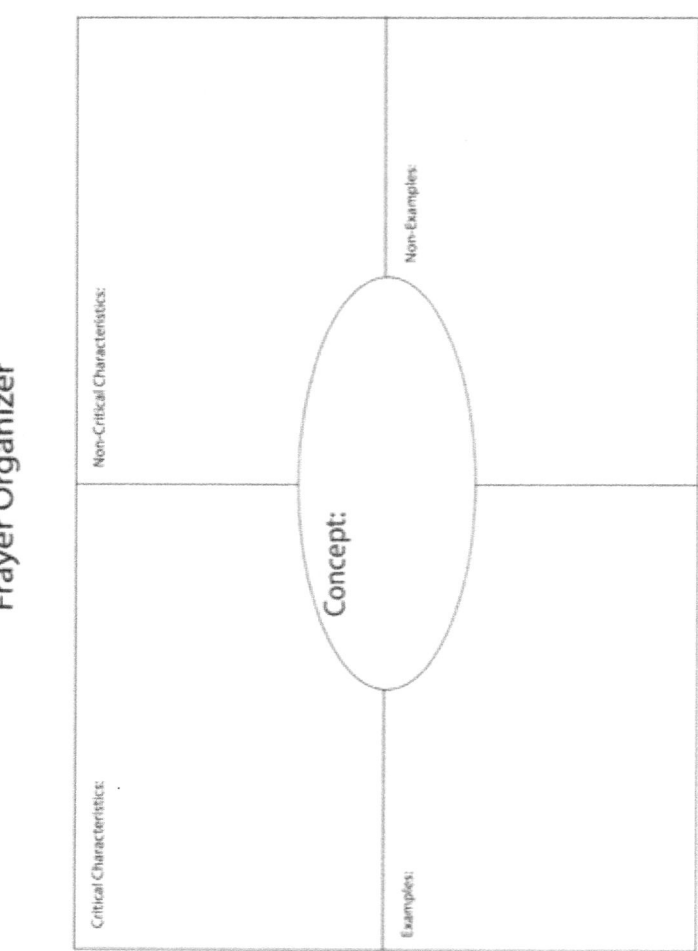

*There are numerous other strategies and graphic organizers, these are samplings of a couple. These are meant to serve you and help you, not limit you. If they're stifling you – don't use them. Use what works for you.*

This is a very elementary organizer for character development. Elaborate once you've determined the basics for a character.

Name: _____     Date: _____

## Create a Character

Basic Facts

Name: _____
Age: _____

3 Character Traits

_____
_____
_____

Where do they live?

Do they live in the past, present, or future? Do they live in the city or country?

_____
_____

**Draw your character**

Write a short history of your character.

_____
_____
_____
_____

A Venn diagram is useful when comparing and contrasting.

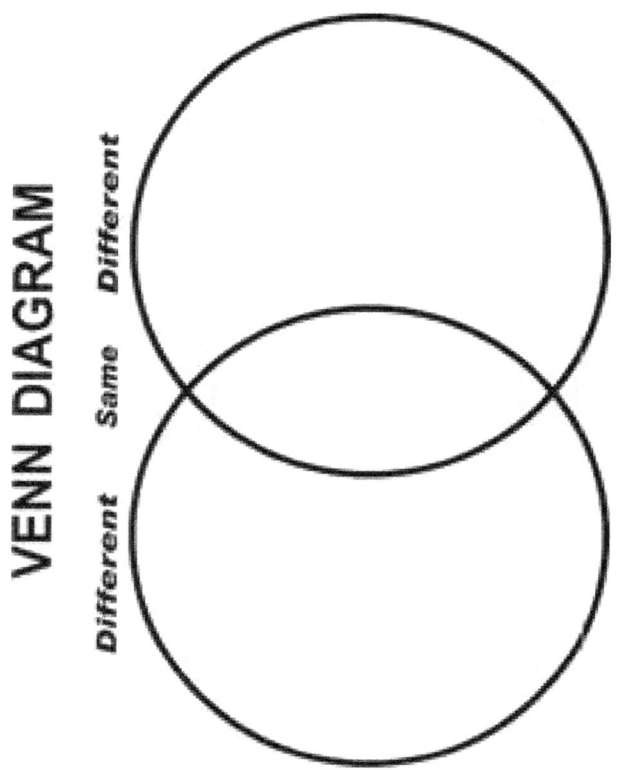

| Different | Same | Different |
|---|---|---|
| Subject A: | Both A & B | Subject B |
| | | |

**14 Literary Devices** (These are just a small sampling of literary devices, not a comprehensive list. Intentionally stretch your writers craft and implement various devices into your writing.)

| Literary Device | Definition | Example |
|---|---|---|
| Allegory | A figure of speech in which abstract ideas and principles are described in terms of characters, figures, and events. It can be used to tell a story, with a purpose of teaching or explaining an idea or a principle. The objective of its use is to teach some kind of a **moral** lesson. | *Pilgrim's Progress* by John Bunyan is a prime example of a literary allegory. |
| Metaphor | A figure of speech in which a term is applied to something to which it is not literally applicable in order to suggest a resemblance. (A metaphor does NOT use the words like or as.) | She is a rose. |
| Simile | A figure of speech in which two unlike things are explicitly compared, using the words 'like' or 'as' | She is like a rose. |
| Analogy | The illustration of one idea by a more familiar or accessible idea that is in some way parallel. | In the same way as one cannot have the rainbow without the rain, one cannot achieve success and riches without hard work. |
| Satire | Satire is a technique employed by writers to expose and criticize foolishness and corruption of an individual or a society, by using humor, exaggeration, ridicule. | "What's the use you learning to do right, when it's troublesome to do right and isn't no trouble to do wrong, and the wages is just the same?" |
| Hyperbole | An obvious, intentional exaggeration for dramatic or comedic effect. | I read a million books this past summer. |

| | | |
|---|---|---|
| Onomatopoeia | A word that sounds like what it means. | Cukoo, meow, honk, boom |
| Alliteration | Two or more nearby words with the same letter or sound. | She sells sea shells by the sea shore. |
| Personification | A figure of speech in which a thing – an idea or an animal – is given human attributes. | The wind whispered through the dry grass. |
| Repetition | Repeating the same words or phrases a few times to make an idea clearer and more memorable. | |
| Round Robin | End in the same way that you began a story or chapter - to bring a story around full circle. | |
| Flashback | The author depicts the occurrence of specific events to the reader, which have taken place before the present time the narration is following, or events that have happened before the events that are currently unfolding in the story. | Back in the day when Sarah was a young girl… |
| Foreshadowing | The use of indicative word or phrases and hints that set the stage for a story to unfold and give the reader a hint of something that is going to happen without revealing the story or spoiling the suspense. Foreshadowing is used to suggest an upcoming outcome to the story. | "He had no idea of the disastrous chain of events to follow". |
| Epilogue | A literary tool that acts as the afterword once the last chapter is over. It adds insight once the plot is over. | |

## Transitional words & phrases

### Examples, support, emphasis

| | | |
|---|---|---|
| in other words | notably | in fact |
| to put it differently | including | in general |
| for one thing | like | in particular |
| as an illustration | to be sure | in detail |
| in this case | namely | for example |
| for this reason | chiefly | for instance |
| to put it another way | truly | to demonstrate |
| | indeed | to emphasize |
| that is to say | certainly | to repeat |
| with attention to | surely | to clarify |
| by all means | markedly | to explain |
| | such as | to enumerate |

### Time, chronology, sequence

| | | |
|---|---|---|
| at the present time | after, next, now | henceforth |
| from time to time | later | whenever |
| sooner or later | last | eventually |
| at the same time | until | meanwhile |
| to begin with | till | further |
| in due time | since | during |
| as soon as | then | in time |
| as long as | before | prior to |
| in the meantime | hence | forthwith |
| in a moment | since | straightaway |
| without delay | when | until now |
| in the first place | once | whenever |
| all of a sudden | about | now that |

| | | |
|---|---|---|
| immediately | formerly | instantly |
| quickly | suddenly | presently |
| finally | shortly | occasionally |

## Space, location, place

| | | |
|---|---|---|
| in the middle | here | further |
| to the left/right | there | beyond |
| in front of | next | nearby |
| on this side | where | wherever |
| in the distance | from | around |
| here and there | over | between |
| in the background | near | before |
| adjacent to | above | alongside |
| opposite to | below | amid, among |

## Opposition, limitation, contradiction

| | | |
|---|---|---|
| although this may be true | but | although |
| in contrast | (and) still | instead |
| different from | unlike | whereas |
| of course ..., but | or | despite |
| on the other hand | (and) yet | conversely |
| on the contrary | while | otherwise |
| at the same time | albeit | however |
| in spite of | besides | rather |
| even so / though | as much as | nevertheless |
| be that as it may | even though | nonetheless |
| then again | | regardless |
| above all | | notwithstanding |

## Grammar Guide

PUNCTUATION

| | |
|---|---|
| Comma , | Used to create a slight pause and/or when listing items |
| Colon : | Used to introduce a list of items |
| Semi-colon ; | Used between 2 independent clauses that could each stand alone as separate sentences. |
| em Dash - | The em **dash** can be used in place of a colon when you want to emphasize the conclusion of your sentence. It is less formal than a semi-colon. |
| Quotation marks " | Used when quoting a text. https://owl.english.purdue.edu/owl/resource/577/03/ |
| Direct quote ' | Inside quotation marks are used for direct quotes of a person speaking. |

Irregular Verbs to Remember

| Verb | Singular form use with: I, he, she | | Plural form use with: you, they, we | |
|---|---|---|---|---|
| | Present tense | Past tense | Present tense | Past tense |
| to be | I am *he/she* is | was was | are | were |
| to have | I have *he/she* has | had had | have | had |
| to do | I do *he/she* does | I did did | do | did |
| to know | I know *he/she* knows | knew knew | know | knew |

Online grammar & writing lab: https://owl.english.purdue.edu/owl/

Grammar cont'd.

1. there – indicating a place. "Please put it over there."
2. their – indicating ownership. "It is their turn."
3. they're – conjugation of the words 'they are'. "They're my friends."

Make note of any grammar rules that may 'trick' you from time to time.

_____
_____
_____
_____
_____
_____
_____
_____
_____
_____
_____
_____
_____
_____
_____
_____
_____
_____
_____
_____
_____
_____
_____
_____
_____
_____
_____
_____
_____
_____

# 4  MUSINGS, DEVOTIONAL & JOURNAL ENTRIES

(Be sure to date your entries.)

_____
_____
_____
_____
_____
_____
_____
_____
_____
_____
_____
_____
_____
_____
_____
_____
_____
_____
_____
_____
_____
_____
_____
_____
_____
_____
_____
_____
_____
_____
_____
_____
_____
_____
_____
_____
_____

Dr. Janet Shuler

# 5   QUOTABLE QUOTES, EXCERPTS & FAVORITE VERSES

Interjecting quotable quotes, short excerpts from other authors and/or Bible verses gives your writing strength, character and depth.

It is helpful to have a 'bank' filled with some of your favorites to serve you whenever needed. (It's also helpful to record the source of the quotes.)

Some like to organize their 'bank' alphabetically or by topic – or simply at random, recording their favorites as they come across them.
Here are some to get you started. Add to your bank regularly.

What are your favorite quotes? Who are some of your favorite authors? I've found profound quotable quotes on social media. (If quoting someone from social media note their name, date, and source, ie; FB, Instagram, Twitter, etc.

## Quotable Quotes
Many but not all of these were used and cited in my book, *Secure the Gates*.

T-i-m-e is a four letter word that spells *LOVE*. – Janet Shuler

Without God you can't without you He won't. – Ed Silvoso

Invincibility lies in the defence; the possibility of victory in the attack.
– Sun Tzu, *The Art of War*

The depth of our character guards our personal gates against deception.
– Janet Shuler

Kindness in words creates confidence. Kindness in thinking creates profoundness. Kindness in giving creates love. – Lao Tzu

The journey of a thousand miles begins with one step. – Lao Tzu

Victorious warriors win first and then go to war, while defeated warriors go to war first and then seek to win. – Sun Tzu, *The Art of War*

The function of education is to teach one to think intensively and critically.

Intelligence plus character – that's the goal of true education. – Martin Luther King, Jr.

We may have all come on different ships, but we're in the same boat now. – Martin Luther King, Jr.

I have decided to stick with love. Hate is too great a burden to bear. – Martin Luther King, Jr.

Love is the only force capable of transforming an enemy into a friend. – Martin Luther King, Jr.

God does not choose men because they are great but makes them great because He has chosen them. - Jonathan Edwards

A world that we do not transform will conform us. – Anonymous

Whether you think you can or think you can't – you're right! – Henry Ford

**Favorite Scriptures**
(Be sure to note which version you are quoting from.)

Therefore he is able to save completely those who come to God through him, because he always lives to intercede for them. (Hebrews 7:25, NIV)

For the creation waits in eager expectation for the children of God to be revealed. (Romans 8:19, NIV)

But you are a chosen people, a royal priesthood, a holy nation, God's special possession, that you may declare the praises of him who called you out of darkness into his wonderful light. Once you were not a people, but now you are the people of God; (1 Peter 2:9-10, NIV)

Anyone who believes in him will never be put to shame. (Romans 10:11, NIV)

The season has changed, the bondage of your barren winter has ended, and the season of hiding is over and gone…. The early signs of my purposes and plans are bursting forth. (Song of Songs 2:11, 13, TPT)

On-goingly enter your favorites. Reference/ credit your sources. *(This will save you a lot of time searching for and crediting sources in your future articles and books.)*

Dr. Janet Shuler

# 6   BECOMING PUBLISHED

Note – *This is not a comprehensive guide to publishing or becoming self published. It is an introductory overview. It is strongly recommended that you do further research and make additional inquiries to decide which options are best for you and understand more fully all that is involved.*

Most budding authors that desire to be published, opt to become self-published.

What is 'self-publishing' and what does it entail?

In traditional publishing the publisher bears the costs of editing, paying in advance, marketing, etc. Self publishing, unlike the traditional publishing model in which control of the publication is shared with a publisher, the author controls the entire process. This includes the design of the cover and the interior, price, distribution, marketing, and public relations. As an author you can do all of these activities or you may outsource these tasks.

A self-publisher also takes on many of the creative tasks to complete the finished works, which include creative writing as well as selecting the writing software, editing, marketing, and cover design.

Most self-publishing platforms offer print on demand (POD).

General Steps to Becoming Published:
Writing
Re-writing
Story-editing
More re-writing
Copyediting
Layout & Typesetting
Cover Design
Purchase an ISBN
Get copyrighted
Select Platforms
Choose Price
Choose Distribution Channels
Upload
Marketing & promotion

Some question the quality and integrity of self-published works, as traditional publishers and editors are sticklers and demand accuracy. Therefore, in order to validate ourselves as self-publishers it is up to us to accurately research facts and properly quote, credit and cite our sources.

For what it is worth, this workbook was done using CreateSpace.)

## Choosing Who to Self Publish With – do it yourself
*a Distribution Platforms comparison chart (2017)*   all are POD

| Criteria | Amazon KDP | Draft2Digital | Lulu | Pronoun |
|---|---|---|---|---|
| User-friendly platform | Very user friendly | Very user friendly | Complicated FAQ | Very user friendly |
| Ease of formatting | Very easy | Very easy | Good | Good |
| Reach & customer satisfaction | Great | Good | Good | Great |
| Free ISBN | Yes | yes | yes | yes |
| In-build cover creator | Yes | No | Yes | No |
| Royalties | Stink | Great | Stink | Great |
| Payment policies | Stink | Good | Good | Good |
| Payment options (PayPal) | Stink | Very good | Very good | Very good |
| other | | | | |
| other | | | | |

Research Additional Distribution Platforms On Your Own:
## Choosing Who to Self Publish With – do it yourself
*a comparison chart (2017)*   all are POD (also: Blurb, Smashwords, Peecho, Lightning Source, Ingram Spark, Gumroad, etc.)

| Criteria | Create Space (dif than KDP) | Kobo | | |
|---|---|---|---|---|
| User-friendly platform | | | | |
| Ease of formatting | | | | |
| Reach & customer satisfaction | | | | |
| Free ISBN | | | | |
| In-build cover creator | | | | |
| Royalties | | | | |
| Payment policies | | | | |
| Payment options (PayPal) | | | | |
| other | | | | |
| other | | | | |

Note – *I am NOT an expert on this topic and markets are changing by the day. The information on these pages is meant to serve as a guide for you to do current research and based upon your findings determine which platform is best for you as an author.*

Visit this site **www.selfpublishingadvice.org**, specifically this page: https://selfpublishingadvice.org/allis-self-publishing-service-directory/self-publishing-service-reviews/ for a critique/
for a comparison chart of best and worst publishing services offered.

So you want to self-publish, but would like a publisher's assistance? That's available too – for a price.
Brace yourself, it's costly and quite the process to go from idea to a published work. (Anywhere from about $1500 to $3500+).

I went with Xulon Press for my first 2 books (*My Bible Counting Book* and *Secure the Gates*). This doesn't make them better or worse – they were what I needed as at the time. Whenever I called I got a real-person that I could talk with to answer my questions. (I hired a prophetic graphic designer, David Munoz, for the cover of *Secure the Gates*. For *My Bible Counting Book*, yours truly did a tempura paint design. I took a picture of it with my cell phone, uploaded and submitted it to the publisher for them to craft in the text and complete the design – which required my approval for publication.)

Before I used the platform of CreateSpace (used for this workbook) I went with a publishing company (Xulon Press) to get published and walk me through the process. It truly was self-publishing as nothing was printed without my approval. (Almost all companies will send you a hard copy or e-publishing guide for free.)

COSTS
There are many publishing companies that work with authors toward self-publishing. The costs for their services on average range between $800 - $3800. Some publishers, offer their services at radically lower prices. You will have to research and compare and contrast which one is right for you.

Also Factor & Budget:
Buying copies of your books (to have on hand for signings and sales) is an additional fee. Some companies charge a larger percentage than others. Be sure to research that. Editing is an additional cost as well. Also, check into services for book cover creation. You're pretty much on your own regarding marketing and promotions.

Choosing a PUBLISHING Company for self-publishing
http://writersweekly.com/compare

| Criteria | Xulon | Xlibris | Ingram Spark | Outskirts Press |
|---|---|---|---|---|
| Cost range | $1500-3800 | $899-$15,000 | | Under $200 |
| Access to a person for Q&A | X | | | |
| They do BISAC description & codes | X | | | |
| Help with marketing & promotion | Available for a price | | | |
| They take care of copyright | X | | | |
| Percentage of Royalties you keep | | | | |
| Cost of editing services | | | | |
| Cost of books | | | | |

## More of your research efforts:

| Criteria | | | | |
|---|---|---|---|---|
| Cost range | | | | |
| Person to person Q&A | | | | |
| They do BISAC description & codes | | | | |
| Help with marketing & promotion | | | | |
| publisher takes care of copyright | | | | |
| Percentage of Royalties you keep | | | | |
| Cost of editing services | | | | |
| Cost of books | | | | |

Editing:

Most self-publishing companies that offer packages do not include comprehensive editing services with your package. The company I went with, Xulon, provided an overview editing service. From their reading of the manuscript that crafted the book summary, BIASC codes for market. They also gave a one page feedback report of the strengths and weaknesses of the manuscript from an editing perspective. In with that was a one sample page from the manuscript marked up with edits.

Editing can be costly. I have not seen editing included in a publishing package. It can be very pricey. In 2017 a self-publishing company gave me a price of 17 cents per word of 30,000 words – which came to $5,100. Yikes!! Then they made me an econo-editing offer of $2500.

If hiring editing services is not in your budget, then have a literate friend or colleague review it. It is helpful for someone with 'fresh eyes' to review it.

Additional Notes to Self:

_____
_____
_____
_____
_____
_____
_____
_____
_____
_____
_____
_____
_____
_____
_____
_____
_____
_____
_____
_____
_____
_____
_____

# 7    MY RESOURCES & REFERENCES

As you have figured out by now – this workbook is meant to be a tool that is relevant to YOU!

Some resources and references have been provided for you to get you started. However you determine how timely and relevant this section will be to you by what you add to it, in an on-going manner.

*(PS) Remember the most valued resources you are divine connections & holy alliances, aka people that God puts in your path and network for His purposes in and through you, on earth as it is in heaven.

To get you started some resources are provided. Add to and organize new additions to this section daily.

| Entry date | Topic | URL |
|---|---|---|
| 3/23/18 | POD price comparison | http://writersweekly.com/compare |
| 3/23/18 | 150 writing resources | http://oedb.org/ilibrarian/150-writing-resources/ |
| 3/23/18 | Fiction university | http://blog.janicehardy.com/ |
| 3/23/18 | Writers Helping Writers Write | http://writershelpingwriters.net/resources-for-writers/ |
| 3/23/18 | The Author's Guild | https://www.authorsguild.org/member-services/writers-resource-library/ |
| 3/23/18 | Style & Voice | http://www.umuc.edu/current-students/learning-resources/writing-center/online-guide-to-writing/tutorial/chapter3/ch3-21.html |
| 3/23/15 | Chicago Manuscript Style Citation Machine | http://www.citationmachine.net/chicago/cite-a-book |

| Internet Resources | | |
|---|---|---|
| **Entry Date** | **Topic** | **URL** |
| | | |
| | | |
| | | |
| | | |
| | | |
| | | |
| | | |
| | | |
| | | |
| | | |
| | | |
| | | |
| | | |

**PEOPLE & Companies**

Name, Address, email, phone #, website

_____
_____
_____
_____
_____
_____
_____
_____
_____
_____
_____
_____
_____
_____
_____
_____
_____
_____
_____
_____
_____
_____
_____
_____
_____
_____
_____
_____
_____
_____
_____
_____
_____
_____
_____
_____
_____

## Books & Magazines
include title, author, publisher, copyright, volume, etc.

_____
_____
_____
_____
_____
_____
_____
_____
_____
_____
_____
_____
_____
_____
_____
_____
_____
_____
_____
_____
_____
_____
_____
_____
_____
_____
_____
_____
_____
_____
_____
_____
_____
_____
_____

# 8   MY WRITING SAMPLES & IDEAS

**Unblocking Writer's Block –**

Writer's block is real, it happens, even to the most prolific of writers. Home run hitters hit slumps and so do writers. Here are 10 tips that will help you unblock the bock in writing:

1. Write anything but write! Keep putting something down on paper.
2. Make mistakes – Give yourself the freedom to make mistakes and be less than perfect. Keep on keeping on!
3. Skip the beginning. The beginning can be the hardest part of your piece. You have the story, its already inside of you. Don't worry about that perfect beginning, skip it! You can come back and skillfully craft it later or another day. Just start writing with what you DO have.
4. Stop in the middle. Some famous authors advocate stopping before you get to the end, while you're still full of juice. This allows you to sleep on it and let it percolate and marinate. The next day you'll be ready to go full steam ahead.
5. Fool yourself. Sometimes the task of writing feels draining or daunting. Tell yourself, "All I have to do is one sentence." Or, "All I have to do is open Word." etc.
6. Limit your writing time. Instead of giving yourself an entire day to write, limit yourself to 2-3 hours.
7. Let it go. Something that isn't working needs to be cut. What's not working? The piece, your approach, the time that you've set aside for writing, the environment, etc. Some things need to be cut or dropped.
8. Change mediums – Switch from a computer to a notebook, from a notebook to a computer, read what you've written aloud, tape yourself reading it and play it back. Perhaps it will shed fresh light and inspiration on the writing.
9. Take a break. Maybe you've just been at it too long and need a break to keep fresh. You know what they say, 'All work and no play, make one boring.' Have fun, enjoy nature, etc.
10. Do what's best for you. If you have epiphany's while jogging speak it into a recording device and transcribe it later. Do what works for you.

Continue writing and add to your current work(s) in progress or copy, cut and paste into this section.

# ABOUT THE AUTHOR

## DR. JANET SHULER

A passionate, prophetic teacher and intercessor, Dr. Janet Shuler is an apostolic leader, spiritual mother, public speaker, webinar presenter, and author. She often travels, ministering to leaders and congregations. Dr. Shuler has also had an extensive career in education (primarily in the public sector), with over 40 years as a: principal, asst. principal, literacy coordinator, staff developer, teacher and adjunct professor for graduate students at Seton Hall University.

Dr. Janet was ordained by Christian International (under Bishop Bill Hamon with Apostles Steven & Dr. Melodye Hilton) and remains under their covering. Other ministries that she co-labors with are: King of Kings under Apostles Peter & Trisha Roselle (associated with Chuck Pierce); Pray for Newark led by Elders Lloyd & Joanne Turner under Apostle Ed Silvoso, Reformation Prayer Network (RPN, under Cindy Jacobs).

Her mission is to establish, equip and empower believers to be an influence for Christ, to be effective in their call and attain their destiny. Dr. Janet works with leaders and their people in building diverse teams; developing powerful, prophetic intercessors, strong leaders, and stable, healthy, believers. Thus establishing those who will reform society, secure gates and lead us into tomorrow.

She honors her husband Jim and is thankful for his love and support. He is the wind beneath her wings. They have 8 adult children + their spouses, and several grandchildren. Family is near and dear to their heart.

**Contact Dr. Janet for ministry bookings, training, activation, and impartation** - receive the Father's heart, with transforming truths!

Invite Dr. Janet to minister & share with your people. Visit our page <u>Courses & Ministry</u> for more information.

Talk with Dr. Janet regarding other areas that you may be interested in. She will work with you to customize topics & teachings based upon your needs and input.

**To learn more about Dr. Janet Shuler or to contact her:**
<u>Contact her by email at</u>:
    HKMdrJanet@gmail.com

<u>Visit her web site at</u>:
    www.jshuler.blog

<u>Follow her on social media at</u>:
FaceBook    www.facebook.com/janetshuler2
Instagram    www.instagram.com/HKMdrJanet

Made in the USA
Middletown, DE
02 December 2018